Great Works
for Piano Four Hands

Edited by Ronald Herder

DOVER PUBLICATIONS, INC.
Mineola, New York

Bibliographical Note

This Dover edition, first published in 1998, is a new compilation of works originally published separately in early authoritative editions. A composite list of contents and new headings have been added, as well as a glossary of French and German terms in the music, specially prepared for this edition.

We are indebted to Professor Peter Kussi, Department of Slavic Languages, Columbia University, New York, for his evaluation of the titles to Janáček's *Moravian Dances*.

International Standard Book Number

ISBN-13: 978-0-486-40173-7
ISBN-10: 0-486-40173-1

Library of Congress Catalog Card Number: 70-107665

Manufactured in the United States by Courier Corporation
40173104   2014
www.doverpublications.com

CONTENTS

LUDWIG VAN BEETHOVEN

Eight Variations on a Theme by Count Waldstein (1792) 2

Sonata in D Major, Op. 6 (1796) 16
   I. Allegro molto   16
   II. Rondo: Moderato   20

Three Marches, Op. 45 (1803) 26
   1. Allegro ma non troppo   26
   2. Vivace   30
   3. Vivace   34

CLAUDE DEBUSSY

Prelude to "The Afternoon of a Faun" (1892–4) 38
   Transcribed by Maurice Ravel

ANTONÍN DVOŘÁK

Six Legends, from Op. 59 (1880–81) 52
   III. Allegro giusto   52
   V. Allegro giusto   60
   VII. Allegretto grazioso   66
   VIII. Un poco Allegretto e grazioso   72
   IX. Andante con moto   80
   X. Andante   84

LEOŠ JANÁČEK

Moravian Dances* (1904) 90
   I. Troják   90
   II. Silnice   90
   III. Tetka   92
   IV. Kukačka   92
   V. Trojky   94
   VI. Starodávný   94
   VII. Kalamajka   96
   VIII. Holubička   96
   IX. Sekerečka   98
   X. Rožek   100
   XI. Konopě   100
   XII. Čeladenský I   102

SERGEI RACHMANINOFF

Barcarolle, Op. 11, No. 1 (1894) 104

Italian Polka (ca. 1906) 116

*Despite a few possible literal translations—"Cuckoo" for "Kukačka"; "Little Dove" for "Holubička," etc.— Janáček's titles generally resist meaningful English equivalents. The original names appear to refer to regional dance types.

MAX REGER

Three Burlesques, from Op. 58 (1901) 124

    III. Ausserst lebhaft, mit Humor   124

    V. Ausserst schnell und flüchtig   132

    VI. So lebhaft und übermütig als nur möglich   138

FLORENT SCHMITT

Reflections of Germany: Waltzes, Op. 28, Book One (1905) 144

    1. Heidelberg   144

    2. Coblentz   152

    3. Lübeck   158

    4. Werder   164

PETER ILYITCH TCHAIKOVSKY

Waltz from the ballet *The Sleeping Beauty*, Op. 66 (1888–9) 168
   Transcribed by Sergei Rachmaninoff

MAURICE RAVEL

Rapsodie Espagnole (1907) 185
   Transcribed by the composer

    I. Prélude à la nuit   185

    II. Malageña   190

    III. Habanera (1895)   195

    IV. Feria   199

GLOSSARY OF FRENCH AND GERMAN TERMS IN THE MUSIC

animé, animated

animez davantage, still livelier

animez légèrement, lightly enliven [the music]

animez sensiblement, appreciably enliven
[the music]

à peine au mouv^t, barely in tempo

assez vif, rather quick

äusserst lebhaft, mit Humor, extremely lively,
with humor

äusserst schnell und flüchtig, extremely swift
and fleeting

au mouv^t [mouvement] = *a tempo*

avec grâce, gracefully

cédez, hold back ("give way")

dans le mouv^t plus animé, in a livelier tempo

dans le 1er mouv^t avec plus de langueur,
resume the first tempo with more listlessness

dessous, beneath [subordinate to another line]

doux et expressif, gentle and expressive

en animant (peu à peu), becoming lively
(little by little)

en dehors, prominent

en demi-teinte et d'un rythme las, half-tinted
and with a weary rhythm

en récit, like a recitative

en s'éloignant, becoming distant

en se perdant, gradually disappearing

erstes Tempo = Tempo I

etwas langsamer, somewhat slower

expressif, expressive

expressivement, expressively

immer langsamer werden, steadily becoming
slower

lent, slow

même mouv^t, the same tempo

modéré(ment), moderate(ly)

moins vite, not as fast

mouv^t du début = [resume] the first tempo

[premier] 1er mouv^t = Tempo I

ralenti, slowed down

ralentissez beaucoup, slow down considerably

retenez (peu à peu), hold back (little by little)

retenu, held back

sans sourdine, unmuted

so lebhaft und übermütig als nur möglich,
as lively and high-spirited as possible

suivez, follow [another part, line or instrument]

toujours en animant, always remaining lively

très animé, very animated

très calme, very calm

très en dehors, very prominent

très expressif et très soutenu, very expressive
and very sustained

très leger, very light

très lent et très retenu jusqu'à la fin, very slow
and very restrained until the end

très modéré, very moderate

un peu attardé, somewhat lagging behind

un peu en dehors, a little to the fore

un peu lent, a bit slow

un peu moins vite, not quite so fast

un peu plus animé, a little livelier

un peu plus moins vite, still less fast [than before]

un peu ralenti, somewhat held back

Footnote, p. 154–155: The sign ⌣ indicates an imperceptible
suspension that serves as a transition, either between loud and
soft dynamics, or between two harmonies, or between two
parts of a phrase, etc.

Great Works
for Piano Four Hands

Eight Variations

on a Theme by Count Waldstein (1792)

Ludwig van Beethoven

SECONDO

Eight Variations
on a Theme by Count Waldstein (1792)

LUDWIG VAN BEETHOVEN

PRIMO

Var.II.

Var.III.

SECONDO

6   Beethoven

SECONDO

SECONDO

PRIMO

Adagio

Tempo I.

Var. VIII.
Un poco Adagio.

calando

Allegro.

SECONDO

PRIMO

SECONDO

Adagio.

Allegretto.

Presto.

Sonata in D Major

Op. 6 (1796)

Ludwig van Beethoven

SECONDO

16

Sonata in D Major

Op. 6 (1796)

LUDWIG VAN BEETHOVEN

PRIMO

18   Beethoven

SECONDO

RONDO.
Moderato.

20   Beethoven

PRIMO

RONDO.
Moderato.

SECONDO

PRIMO

SECONDO

24   Beethoven

PRIMO

Three Marches

Op. 45 (1803)

LUDWIG VAN BEETHOVEN

SECONDO

Nº 1.

Allegro ma non troppo.

Three Marches

Op. 45 (1803)

LUDWIG VAN BEETHOVEN

PRIMO

N.º 1.

Allegro ma non troppo.

SECONDO

Marcia D. C.

№ 2.

№ 2.

PRIMO

Vivace.

SECONDO

PRIMO

SECONDO

Vivace.

Nº 3.
Vivace.

SECONDO

D. C. senza Repetizione sin' al Fine

D. C. senza Repetizione sin'al Fine

Prelude to "The Afternoon of a Faun"

Prélude à "L'aprés-midi d'un faune"

(1892–4)

Transcribed for piano four hands
by Maurice Ravel

CLAUDE DEBUSSY

SECONDO

Prelude to "The Afternoon of a Faun"

Prélude à "L'aprés-midi d'un faune"

(1892–4)

Transcribed for piano four hands
by Maurice Ravel

CLAUDE DEBUSSY

PRIMO

SECONDO

40 Debussy

PRIMO

SECONDO

PRIMO

SECONDO

PRIMO

SECONDO

Six Legends

from [10] *Legends*, Op. 59 (1880–81)

SECONDO

III.

Antonín Dvořák

Allegro giusto. ♩ = 120.

Six Legends

from [10] *Legends*, Op. 59 (1880–81)

PRIMO

III.

ANTONÍN DVOŘÁK

53

SECONDO

54   Dvořák

PRIMO

SECONDO

PRIMO

SECONDO

58 Dvořák

PRIMO

V.

PRIMO

V.

SECONDO

SECONDO

PRIMO

VII.

Allegretto grazioso. ♩=84.

VII.

Allegretto grazioso. ♩=84.

SECONDO

Poco più mosso.

68 Dvořák

Poco più mosso.

PRIMO

VIII.

PRIMO

VIII.

PRIMO

Tempo. ♩. = 72.

Un poco meno mosso. PRIMO

SECONDO

PRIMO

IX.

IX.

Tempo I.

X.

X.

SECONDO

PRIMO

Moravian Dances

(1904)

LEOŠ JANÁČEK

SECONDO

I. Troják

II. Silnice

Moravian Dances
(1904)

Leoš Janáček

PRIMO
I. Troják

II. Silnice

III. Tetka

IV. Kukačka

III. Tetka

IV. Kukačka

V. Trojky

VI. Starodávný

V. Trojky

VI. Starodávný

VII. Kalamajka

VIII. Holubička

VII. Kalamajka

VIII. Holubička

SECONDO

IX. Sekerečka

IX. Sekerečka

Con moto ♩=144

X. Rožek

XI. Konopě

X. Rožek

XI. Konopě

XII. Čeladenský I.

XII. Čeladenský I.

Barcarolle

No. 1 from *Six Pieces*, Op. 11 (1894)

Sergei Rachmaninoff

SECONDO

Barcarolle

No. 1 from *Six Pieces*, Op. 11 (1894)

SERGEI RACHMANINOFF

PRIMO

SECONDO

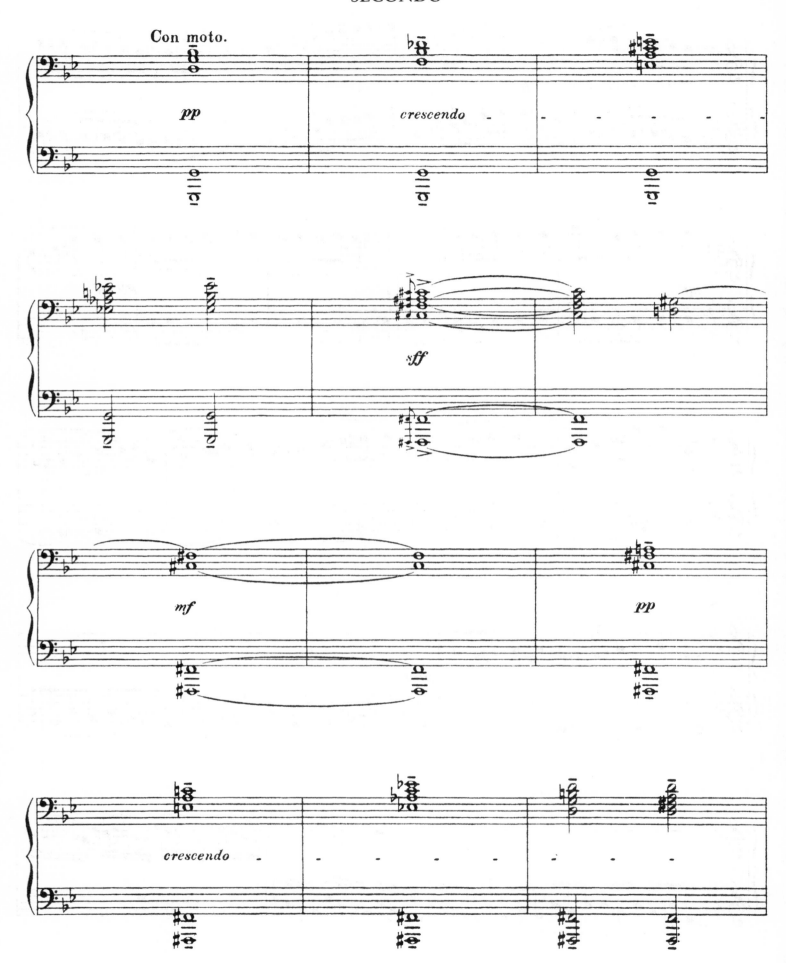

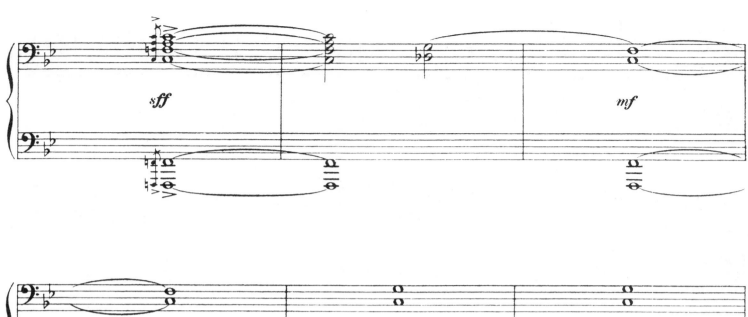

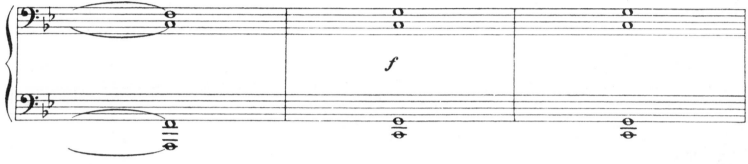

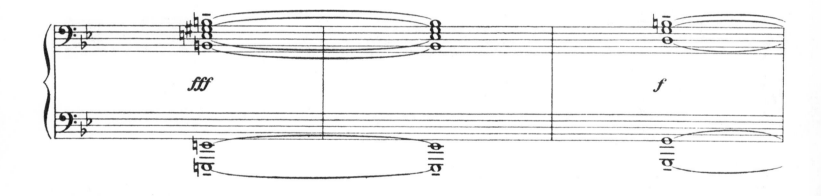

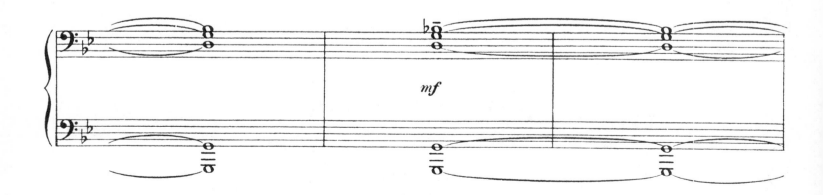

SECONDO

Italian Polka
(ca. 1906)

SERGEI RACHMANINOFF

SECONDO

Italian Polka

(ca. 1906)

Sergei Rachmaninoff

PRIMO

SECONDO

SECONDO

Three Burlesques

from *Six Burlesques*, Op. 58 (1901)

SECONDO

III.

MAX REGER

124

Three Burlesques

from *Six Burlesques*, Op. 58 (1901)

PRIMO

III.

MAX REGER

Äusserst lebhaft, mit Humor

SECONDO

PRIMO

PRIMO

SECONDO

PRIMO

f *e* *sempre* *poco* *a* *poco* *cre* -

- - - -scen - - - - - - - -

- - - -do - - - *fff*

assai marc. *sempre fff*

ffz *ffz* *ffz* *ffz*

V.

Äusserst schnell und flüchtig

Etwas langsamer

PRIMO

V.

Äusserst schnell und flüchtig

SECONDO

SECONDO

PRIMO

VI.

So lebhaft und übermütig als nur möglich

VI.

So lebhaft und übermütig als nur möglich

PRIMO

SECONDO

Reflections of Germany: Waltzes

Reflets d'Allemagne: Valses, Op. 28, Book One (1905)

FLORENT SCHMITT

SECONDO

To Messieurs Claude and Jean Forestier

1. Heidelberg

Reflections of Germany: Waltzes

Reflets d'Allemagne: Valses, Op. 28, Book One (1905)

FLORENT SCHMITT

PRIMO

To Messieurs Claude and Jean Forestier

1. Heidelberg

SECONDO

SECONDO

PRIMO

SECONDO

To Monsieur and Madame Paul Arosa

2. Coblentz

To Monsieur and Madame Paul Arosa

2. Coblentz

SECONDO

PRIMO

(1) ⏜ indique une suspension imperceptible pour servir de transition soit entre le **ff** et le **pp**, soit entre deux harmonies, soit encore entre deux membres d'une phrase, etc...

SECONDO

SECONDO

To Madame Armand Bernard

3. Lübeck

To Madame Armand Bernard

3. Lübeck

PRIMO

SECONDO

To Jean Tavernier

4. Werder

To Jean Tavernier

4. Werder

SECONDO

Waltz

from the ballet *The Sleeping Beauty*, Op. 66 (1888–9)

Transcribed for piano four hands
by Sergei Rachmaninoff

PETER ILYITCH TCHAIKOVSKY

SECONDO

Waltz

from the ballet *The Sleeping Beauty*, Op. 66 (1888–9)

Transcribed for piano four hands
by Sergei Rachmaninoff

PETER ILYITCH TCHAIKOVSKY

PRIMO

PRIMO

PRIMO

176   Tchaikovsky

PRIMO

SECONDO

SECONDO

PRIMO

Rapsodie Espagnole

Spanish Rhapsody (1907)

Transcribed for piano four hands
by the composer

MAURICE RAVEL

I. Prélude à la nuit
Prelude to the Night

II. Malagueña

III. Habanera

(1895)

IV. Feria
Fair

204   Ravel

END OF EDITION